YOU AND YOUR PET
DOGS

YOU AND YOUR PET
DOGS

PHIL STEINBERG

Illustrations by SCOTT W. EARLE

Lerner Publications Company
Minneapolis

Front cover photo by Claudine Marechal.
Back cover photo by Klaus Paysan.

LIBRARY OF CONGRESS CATALOGING IN PUBLICATION DATA

Steinberg, Phillip Orso.
Dogs.

(You and Your Pet)
Includes index.
SUMMARY: Discusses dogs and puppies as pets including information about breeds, feeding, grooming, general health, and training.

1. Dogs—Juvenile literature. [1. Dogs] I. Earle, Scott W.
II. Title. III. Series.

SF426.5.S74 1978   636.7   78-54354
ISBN 0-8225-1253-X

Copyright © 1978 by Lerner Publications Company

All rights reserved. International copyright secured. No part of this book may be reproduced in any form whatsoever without permission in writing from the publisher except for the inclusion of brief quotations in an acknowledged review.

Manufactured in the United States of America. Published simultaneously in Canada by J. M. Dent & Sons (Canada) Ltd., Don Mills, Ontario.

International Standard Book Number: 0-8225-1253-X
Library of Congress Catalog Card Number: 78-54354

2 3 4 5 6 7 8 9 10 85 84 83 82 81 80

CONTENTS

Introduction	7
The Origin of the Dog	8
How the Dog Was Domesticated	8
Breeds of Dogs	10
The Right Dog for You	17
The First Day with Your Puppy	28
Housebreaking	36
Training Your Puppy	39
Your Dog's Health	45
Feeding Your Dog	50
Grooming Your Dog	52
When Your Dog Has Puppies	56
Conclusion	60
Index	62

INTRODUCTION

Some dog owners think that their pets are people. Even though dogs do such nonhuman things as wag their tails and pant, their expressive eyes, intelligent responses, and friendly natures make them seem almost human. Dogs are easily able to adapt to humans and become part of the human world, and perhaps this is one of their most remarkable qualities. Dogs love people, and most people are glad that they do.

Because dogs in their natural state live in groups, they instinctively seek companionship and respond to a leader. A human leader is as welcome as one of their own kind. Because dogs can readily respond to human commands, they have become popular not only as work animals but also as companions and pets. Today about one out of every three families in the United States owns at least one dog. In total, about 25 million dogs have won places in human families.

Because dogs want companionship—just ask any dog owner—they will comfort you when you are lonely, welcome you home when you are tired, and protect you from dangers real and imagined. Dogs are friends you can rely on.

THE ORIGIN OF THE DOG

The dog, like the cat, is descended from a prehistoric animal called *Miacis* (MY-uh-sis). This animal lived some 40 million years ago and was the size of a skunk. It had short legs and a long body and tail. It was probably a tree-climber. Some of *Miacis'* descendants developed into cat-like animals. Others were ancestors of the bear. Still others developed into *Cynodictis* (sin-oh-DICK-tis), nature's first link to the modern dog.

Among the animals that developed from *Cynodictis* was *Tomarctus* (toe-MARK-toos). It lived about 15 million years ago. Many scientists believe that this is the animal from which the modern dog is descended. We definitely know that *Tomarctus* was the ancestor of jackals, wolves, foxes, and other dog-like animals. This group of animals makes up a family called *Canidae* (KAH-nih-die), a Latin word that means "canine" (dog-like).

HOW THE DOG WAS DOMESTICATED

Scientists tell us that the dog was the first animal to be domesticated. This happened more than 20,000 years ago, long before the cat was domesticated by the Egyptians. We can only guess how the dog developed into a companion for humans. It may have happened something like this.

Perhaps some prehistoric people found a litter of baby

jackals deserted by the mother. They may have brought the jackals home with the idea of fattening them up for a meal. But their children may have found that the jackal pups were fun to play with. As the pups and the children grew up together, they became friends. Then, by chance, the prehistoric people may have discovered that the jackals protected their homes from wild animals and from other people. Later, they may have learned that the jackals' keen sense of smell could be used to track animals for food.

Prehistoric people no doubt realized the advantages of this partnership with jackals. They may have thought that if a small jackal could guard and hunt for humans, a larger animal could do the same jobs better. This idea may have sent hunters out in search of wolf litters to bring home. As the wolf pups grew tame, they proved to be better guards than the jackals. The wolves' sense of smell, however, was not as keen as that of the jackals.

Sharing the same home, the jackals and wolves eventually mated and produced an animal almost as large as the wolf with a nose as keen as the jackal's. All modern dogs are probably descended from the offspring of these early wolves and jackals.

BREEDS OF DOGS

As human beings scattered themselves over the earth, they took their dogs with them. And as humans adapted to different climates and different jobs, they bred their dogs to do the same.

Breeds are closely related groups of animals that have been developed through controlled mating. "Controlled mating" means that individual dogs with special, desirable characteristics are mated so that their offspring will have these characteristics, too. For the most part, special breeds of dogs were developed by people who wanted dogs for particular jobs. Large, brave dogs, such as mastiffs and Great Danes, were bred to be

Scottish Terrier

watchdogs. Dogs with an exceptionally keen sense of smell and great speed, such as whippets and greyhounds, were bred for hunting. Smaller hunting dogs were needed to dig out burrowing badgers and rabbits. For this purpose, the short-legged terriers and dachshunds were developed. Dogs such as Alaskan malamutes and Siberian huskies were bred for endurance in cold climates. Collies were bred for herding sheep.

    No other mammal has been bred into so many varieties as the dog. Nor does any domestic animal perform so many different jobs. In the mountains of Switzerland, the Saint Bernard was bred to rescue people lost in snowstorms. Other kinds of large dogs were bred to pull small carts in Holland and Belgium. Bloodhounds still find lost children and escaped criminals, and "seeing-eye" dogs guide the blind.

Humans learned to appreciate the dog's loyalty and faithfulness as well as its ability to perform a job. People who did not hunt sometimes obtained hunting dogs as companions and friends. When dogs became house pets, people began to breed them solely for the purpose of developing better pets. Through selective breeding, the "toy" dog, or lapdog, was produced. Because of its size, the toy dog became a favorite pet for those living in crowded cities. The toy does not need the room a larger dog should have, nor does it need the daily exercise a larger dog requires. Except for the fact that toy and miniature breeds are smaller than other breeds, they possess all the qualities of their larger cousins.

In the 1800s people became so interested in the dog's beauty and intelligence that they began displaying their pets in dog shows. The first official dog show took place in England in 1859. Eleven years later, dog shows were held in the United States. As a result of the first shows, dog fanciers formed dog clubs, of which the American Kennel Club remains the most popular. The clubs established rules for judging the various breeds. The rules set standards for judging not only the dog's appearance but also its ability to perform in tests called "obedience trials." The exercises in the trials were designed to teach dogs good manners, thereby making them better pets and companions.

The American Kennel Club recognizes more than 120 breeds of dogs for show competition. These breeds are divided into six groups: sporting dogs, hounds, working dogs, terriers, toy dogs, and non-sporting dogs.

Sporting dogs are bred to help hunters. They are used for locating prey, flushing it out into the open, and bringing it back to the hunter after it has been shot. Sporting dogs include pointers, retrievers, spaniels, setters, and weimaraners. Sporting dogs are often referred to as gun dogs.

Hounds are the hunters of the dog family. There are two kinds of hound dogs: one kind uses its eyesight for tracking, and the other kind uses its sense of smell. Of the hounds, the beagle is the best known of the scent-tracking dogs. Other scent trackers are bassets, dachshunds, and bloodhounds. Of all dogs, the bloodhound has the keenest sense of smell. The hounds that use their eyesight for tracking are greyhounds, wolfhounds, and whippets.

Working dogs are bred to perform various jobs. Some pull carts, some do police work, some herd animals, and some lead the blind. This group of dogs includes Alaskan malamutes, boxers, collies, Great Danes, Saint Bernards, Doberman pinschers, and German shepherds.

Terriers are smaller hunting dogs bred for entering burrows and digging out small animals, such as badgers and rabbits. This group includes fox terriers, Scottish terriers, and Welsh terriers. The miniature schnauzer is also a member of the terrier group. Terriers are very active and hardy. Most make ideal house pets.

Toy dogs are small dogs bred to be companions and pets. Many members of this group have been around for a long time. The Maltese, a small dog from Malta, has enjoyed pet status for more than 2,800 years. The smallest of the toy breeds is the Chihuahua. An especially small Chihuahua can fit in a pocket. The Pekingese is a toy dog that was bred in China more than 2,000 years ago. This fluffy pet was first used for warming its owner's hands. Other toy breeds include pugs, toy poodles, Yorkshire terriers, and miniature pinschers. Toy dogs make excellent pets for people who live in close quarters. But some toys tend to be nervous and excitable.

Non-sporting dogs are dogs that were once hunters and working dogs but are now house pets. This group includes the standard poodle and the dalmation. Because the poodle learns tricks faster than most dogs, it is the dog most often used in the circus. The dalmation is a non-sporting dog, adopted as a mascot by fire fighters years ago. Other non-sporting dogs are bulldogs, chow chows, and Boston terriers.

Among all the varieties of dogs recognized by the American Kennel Club, 10 breeds are favored by the owners of purebred dogs in this country. The popularity of the various breeds changes from time to time. In 1953 Irish setters ranked only 26th among the breeds, and Saint Bernards were 38th. Twenty years later the Saint Bernard ranked 7th in popularity and the Irish setter rose to 3rd place. In 1953 the poodle was 10th on the list of dog favorites. In 1973 it was America's first choice.

Some of the most popular breeds today are: poodle, German shepherd, Irish setter, beagle, dachshund, miniature schnauzer, Saint Bernard, Doberman pinscher, labrador retriever, and cocker spaniel.

THE RIGHT DOG FOR YOU

Choosing a dog is a serious undertaking. You and your parents must understand that owning a dog is a great responsibility requiring some sacrifices. A puppy may wet on the floor. As it grows up, it may chew the draperies or scratch the furniture. It may dig in the lawn, or disturb the neighbors with its barking. Dog food costs money and so do visits to the veterinarian. Boarding your pet at a kennel or finding a friend to care for it while you are away from home is a bothersome task. And someone must take a dog for a walk in all kinds of weather. It is only fair that you and your family are aware of the negative aspects of having a dog. Now you are ready to ask: Are my family and I willing to accept the responsibilities of owning a dog?

Miniature Schnauzer

Old English Sheepdog

Many people who have never owned a dog think that to take on another responsibility, another mouth to feed, another burden, does not make sense. But these people know nothing of the love and companionship a dog provides. They do not know that owning a dog can be the most enriching and unforgettable experience a girl or boy can have. These nonbelievers do not realize that human beings *need* pets. Specialists interested in the mental and emotional health of young people realize the important part a dog plays in a child's life. A dog is a friend who is always there. And owning a dog teaches a child responsibility and consideration not only for his or her pet but also for other human beings.

Mixed-Breed or Purebred?

If you have decided that you are ready to own a dog, then the next question you must ask yourself is: Do I want a mixed-breed or a purebred dog? Purebred dogs have family histories called "pedigrees." Most purebreds are registered with the American Kennel Club. Their pedigrees tell the names of the dog's parents and grandparents. A purebred is more likely to have the same physical appearance and disposition that its parents and grandparents had, which is one of the advantages of owning a purebred. You will know in advance what size dog your puppy will be and what it will look like when it is grown.

Pedigree certificate

Poodle (sire)

Cocker Spaniel (dam)

Cockapoo (offspring)

Mixed-breed dogs, sometimes called "mongrels" or "mutts," have unknown family histories. Each one has its own characteristics. A small mongrel puppy may grow up to be the same size as its father (sire), or it may take after its mother (dam). You're never quite sure what a mixed-breed pup will look like until it becomes an adult dog. A special kind of a mixed-breed dog is a half-breed, which is produced by crossbreeding purebred dogs of two different breeds. For instance, if a poodle and a cocker spaniel mate, the offspring are half poodle and half cocker, and are called "cockapoos." Such half-breed dogs are becoming quite popular.

Of course, purebreds cost a lot more than mixed breeds. You must realize, however, that the price you pay for any puppy is just a small part of the total cost of owning a dog. A large mongrel will eat as much as a large purebred. And all dogs need shots and periodic visits to the veterinarian. It costs as much to own a mongrel as it does to own a purebred—only the initial cost is different. A mongrel pup can be purchased from a pet shop or from the Humane Society for as little as $15. A purebred pup can cost between $35 and $300, depending upon its breed and pedigree. Some pups from champion dams and sires sell for more than a thousand dollars.

Just because mixed breeds cost less than purebreds does not mean that they are inferior. More than half of all house dogs in the United States are of a mixed breed. Many owners of mongrels believe that dogs of a mixed breed make better pets. Certain breeds of purebred dogs tend to be high-strung and nervous. Crossbreeding usually eliminates these tendencies.

Other undesirable traits may appear in purebred dogs if they are bred improperly. In order to keep up with the demand for a popular breed of dog, some greedy breeders will mate brothers and sisters. This inbreeding produces puppies that have physical disorders and bad temperaments. To avoid this problem, purebred pups should be purchased only from reliable breeders. The puppies should have three-generation pedigree papers registered with the American Kennel Club.

If you decide to purchase a purebred pup, I suggest you visit an all-breed dog show before making your choice. At a dog show you can see the various breeds and compare them. You will also have a chance to talk to some of the dog owners. They will gladly answer any questions you may have. They can give you the names of reliable breeders, and they also can tell you which breed of dog is suited for you and your surroundings.

Before choosing your dog, consider its size when it is fully grown. Very large dogs, such as Saint Bernards, Great Danes, and Irish setters, need a lot of space for running. They are not recommended for people who live in the city. Some large dogs, such as German shepherds, Doberman pinschers, and collies, do get along very well in the city if they are given daily exercise. For people living in small homes or apartments, miniature and toy dogs make the best pets. They eat less and are easier to clean up after. They take up less space and do not need as much exercise as large dogs.

If you choose a mixed-breed dog, you will have fun trying to guess its family history. You can do this by comparing the looks of your dog with those of the purebreds. Get a book from the library showing pictures of the different breeds.

Each breed has certain noticeable characteristics. If the mongrel you choose has a long jaw, its ancestors may have been shepherds, greyhounds, or Irish setters. If the jaw is short, your pup could be related to the Saint

Bernard, chow chow, or Chihuahua, depending on its size. The number of teeth a dog has also gives a clue. Most adult dogs have 42 teeth, but German shepherds and Doberman pinschers have a few less. The size and shape of the ears and the length of the hair may also offer clues to your dog's ancestry.

  Study the actions of your dog. Does the dog keep its nose to the ground? It could be of bloodhound, beagle, or basset ancestry. If your dog likes swimming, it may be related to retrievers or spaniels.

You may never discover the true ancestry of your mixed-breed dog, but trying to find out will help you to understand the habits and appearances of the various breeds. And you will come to realize that a dog can be a good companion, whether it is one breed or a combination of breeds.

Purebred or mixed breed? The choice is up to you. Whatever dog you choose, you are sure to love it and enjoy its companionship for many years.

Male or Female?

The next question to ask yourself is: Do I want a male or female dog? A female dog is usually more affectionate than a male. She will stay closer to home and will not be as excitable as a male. Of course, if you intend to raise and sell puppies, you will choose a female. If you don't want your dog to have babies, you can have her *spayed.* This is a simple operation performed by a veterinarian. Spayed females make excellent family pets.

Male dogs are usually livelier than females. Because they grow larger and stronger than females, they make better watchdogs. Males, however, are often more difficult to housebreak. Because of their strong sexual instincts, they tend to roam and get into fights more than females. The urge to look for females can be changed in male dogs by a simple operation called "neutering." A neutered male spends more time at home. He is more interested in you than in finding female dogs. Neutering helps make a dog a better pet. If your purebred male dog is an exceptionally fine animal, you may want to use him for breeding purposes. In that case, of course, you would not have him neutered.

Male or female? Once again, it is up to you to decide. Both sexes make good pets.

THE FIRST DAY WITH YOUR PUPPY

A puppy should be adopted when it is between 6 and 12 weeks old. At this age it is ready to leave its mother and begin eating solid foods. (This process is called "weaning.") It is ready to start a new life in your home. But you and your family must realize that a puppy is still a baby. For a few days it will need special attention and care.

Plan to bring the puppy home early on a Saturday morning. By doing so, you will have an entire weekend to get acquainted with your new pet and to give it the attention it needs. Let the people who sell you the pup know when you are coming to pick it up. Tell them not to give it any breakfast. This will lessen the possibility of the puppy becoming carsick on the ride home. But keep a large towel handy anyway.

On the trip home, hold the puppy on your lap. This will give it a chance to get used to your particular smell. Smells are very important to dogs; they use their noses more than they use their eyes. If you must travel a great distance from the breeder to your home, stop occasionally so that the puppy can stretch its legs and relieve itself.

The arrival of a new puppy is an exciting, happy event. It is natural that you should want all your friends to see the cute pup the day you bring it home. But this is not a good idea. The puppy must adjust to its new home and newly acquired family. Seeing and smelling too many people the first day will only confuse and frighten the animal. It should be given every chance to get settled without too much excitement.

The puppy should be confined to one room of the house until it is completely housebroken. The kitchen is probably the best room. Its tile or linoleum floor is easy to keep clean, and the back door usually is located near the kitchen. The puppy should be taken outside once every hour for the first few days. For this reason, it is wise to adopt your dog while the weather is mild. Puppies old enough to be weaned can be taken outside in all kinds of weather. Their thick fur keeps them warm. But *you* may not feel like going out in the cold and snow. Putting on a heavy coat and overshoes every hour can become an unpleasant chore.

Another reason why the kitchen is the best room for your puppy is that it is used a lot by the whole family. There, your puppy and your family can get to know each other. Human contact is important to a young dog. It is never too early to start developing love and companionship between you and your dog. The attachment of a dog to its owner takes place quickly, usually within a few days. This "sealing of the bond" makes training easier and more enjoyable for you and your dog.

As the owner of a dog, you must see that your pet is properly cared for. It is your duty to see that the animal is not mistreated by young children; do not let them pull the puppy's tail or pick it up by its front legs. The proper way to pick up a puppy is to cup your hands under its stomach and hind legs. Support the puppy but do not squeeze it.

Puppies love to play, and they are fun to play with. But puppies need a lot of rest. Do not force your pup to play if it is tired or sleepy. Put the puppy in its box so that it can take a nap and get used to its bed.

For the first few days, you should feed your puppy the food it is used to eating. Then, if you wish, you can gradually change its diet. A frisky pup burns up a lot of energy. It should be fed five times a day. Feeding is easier if a dish of dry puppy chow is always available alongside a dish of water. The puppy will eat whenever it is hungry. Your pup may appear fat and roly-poly, but that is the way a healthy puppy should look. As it grows older, the puppy fat will disappear.

The first night or two will be difficult for you and your puppy. Your pet will be lonely and will cry for your atten-

tion. But that is the time to make a strict set of rules for yourself and your family, and to see that no one breaks them. Although it may seem cruel, the first rule is to ignore the puppy at night. Do not give in to its crying. If you do, you are in for a lot of trouble. A puppy forms habits quickly. It will cry every night if it knows that you will come running. This makes training and housebreaking almost impossible.

Instead of giving in to your puppy's crying, put a piece of your worn clothing in its bed. Your smell will give the pup a feeling of security. A ticking alarm clock placed next to its bed will remind it of its mother's heartbeat and lull it to sleep.

If the puppy keeps the family awake all night with its howling, roll up a newspaper and slap it loudly against the bed. The noise probably will scare it into being quiet.

The puppy then will know that you are the boss and that you do not like its howling. Be firm with your puppy, and do not pamper it. This may seem a cruel way to treat a lonely puppy, but, in the long run, it is best for you and best for your pet.

Your first days and nights with your puppy are important. They set the standards by which you will raise your dog. It is never too early to begin teaching your pet good manners. If it plays too roughly or bites, gently slap it under the jaw with a rolled-up newspaper and scold it. Teach it early to know what the word "no" means. But be just as quick to praise and reward it when it does the right thing. "Good dog" are the words your puppy will love to hear. Affection along with discipline will turn your puppy into a good house pet. An obedient dog is happy because it knows how to make its owner happy.

While your puppy was still drinking its mother's milk, it was receiving natural protection against various diseases. Once it was weaned, it quickly lost this protection. Therefore, within a week of weaning, a veterinarian should see your puppy. The doctor will examine the pup to make sure it is in good health and does not have worms. The puppy will receive shots to protect it from diseases such as distemper, hepatitis, and rabies, which can be fatal. Puppy vaccinations will protect your dog until it is three months old. At that age the animal will be given adult shots. Booster shots once a year will continue to protect your pet.

HOUSEBREAKING

To housebreak a puppy means to teach it to control its bladder and bowels until it gets outside. Different people have different ideas on how to housebreak a puppy. Some believe in waiting until the puppy is three months old. I believe in beginning training the minute the puppy comes home. Some dog owners think training should begin by teaching the puppy to eliminate on newspapers. This method prolongs the training period and makes extra work for you. Perhaps paper training is all right for miniature and toy dogs, but for larger dogs it should be avoided. Some people believe it takes three months to housebreak a puppy. I know it can be done in less than a week.

By instinct, the dog is a clean animal. The wild ancestors of the dog lived in dens. They always went outside to relieve themselves so that they would not dirty their dens. Cows and birds are not den-dwellers; they cannot be housebroken. But dogs can be trained because their den-dwelling instincts tell them not to make a mess in their own living space.

The time it takes you to housebreak your puppy will depend upon the method you use and the amount of special attention you devote to your dog. The secret of successful housebreaking is anticipating your puppy's needs in time to take it outside. It should not get in the habit of using the house as a bathroom. The puppy should be taken outside as soon as it wakes up, before and after play, after every nap, after each meal, and just before you go to bed. For the first few days this means going outside once every hour. Pick one particular spot in the yard for the puppy to use. This will keep it from ruining your lawn when it grows up, and you will have an easier time cleaning up the area.

The spot that you choose in your yard should be prepared in advance. To do this, mop up the puppy's first mistake with a rag. Put the rag on the spot you have chosen and weight it down with a rock or a brick. The smell of the rag will attract the puppy. Soon it will be in the habit of using just this spot as a bathroom. Stay with the puppy until it relieves itself. Praise your pet and let it know how pleased you are. There is nothing a dog wants more than to hear praise from its master.

A weaned puppy is old enough to control itself the entire night, and it will do so if confined to its "den." I housebroke my dog, Zipper, in less than a week with the "den method." Before I brought Zipper home, I built a special den-bed for him. It was a box in which he could stretch out full length. The top and sides of the box had several holes for ventilation. I made Zipper take all his naps in the box so that he would learn that it was his bed. After each nap I opened the door of the box and immediately took Zipper outside. I did not give him any food or water in the evening, and I made sure that he relieved himself outside before I locked him in his den-bed for the night. He never soiled his bed. Within a week he was used to controlling himself all night. From then on I left the door to his bed open at all times.

This way of housebreaking takes advantage of the dog's instinct to respect its den. The box must be shallow and small to prevent the dog from soiling one part of it and sleeping in another. The "den method" has worked for me and for thousands of other dog owners. Try it. It's a fast and simple way to housebreak your puppy.

TRAINING YOUR PUPPY

A dog must be six months old before it can go to obedience training school. But you can and should teach your puppy simple obedience soon after it is housebroken. This training will prevent the puppy from forming bad habits that are difficult to correct. These lessons will require a lot of patience from you. They must be repeated over and over until the young dog understands exactly what you want it to do.

"Stay," "sit," and "shake hands" are strange words to a puppy. It will need time to learn your language, so have patience. In training a dog, praise and affectionate petting do more good than scolding and punishment. Because a puppy is easily distracted, work with your pet no more than 10 minutes at one time and give it plenty of playtime between lessons.

The first command to teach your puppy is "stay." To do this, put a treat in front of it and hold the palm of your left hand in front of its face. In a stern but quiet voice, say "stay." Each time it goes for the treat, push the dog back and say "stay." Wait a minute before saying "okay," and then let the dog eat the treat. Now praise the pup and pet it. Do this several times. Your pup will learn that it

"Sit"

"Stay"

must not eat the treat until you give the command. And it will learn to stand perfectly still every time it hears you say "stay." Soon the mere sight of you holding up your left hand will stop the dog in its tracks. This is called silent command and is a very important part of obedience training.

The next command to teach your dog is "sit." To do this, tell it to stay. Then walk behind the dog. Say "sit" and, at the same time, push down on the dog's rump as you pull back on its collar. Hold the dog in this position as you repeat the word "sit." Now praise and pet the dog. Do this repeatedly. The dog will soon sit on command.

Many people think shaking hands is just a cute dog trick. Actually, it is a lesson in good manners. A dog should not be allowed to jump on people. Shaking hands is a much better way for a dog to greet guests. When a friend comes to your house, ask him or her to hold out a hand and make a fist. Give your dog a chance to sniff the guest's fist. Then ask your pet to shake hands. Your friend will appreciate your dog's good manners.

To teach your dog to shake hands, command it to stay and to sit. Kneel in front of it. Then tap the back of its right front leg with your hand. When your pet lifts its paw, take it in your hand and say "shake hands." Praise

"Good dog" *"Shake"*

the dog and show your affection. Do this over and over until the dog automatically lifts its right paw every time you say "shake" or "shake hands."

By the time your dog learns to stay, sit, and shake hands, it also will know how to give you its full attention. And through your praise and affection, it will know the joy of pleasing its owner. Teaching the dog simple tricks will be quite easy.

Dogs love to perform tricks. You may want to teach your dog how to sit up, fetch, roll over, and speak. Use plenty of patience, repetition, and praise. Always make the dog think it has done a good job even if its performance is less than perfect; dogs do not like to be failures. If your pet has trouble with a new trick, have it perform a trick it already knows. Smile, say "good dog," and pet it. The dog is then ready to try the new trick once again.

As your pup grows older you will want to teach it to walk by your side. This is called "heeling." You will also want to teach it to come when you call its name. This training enables you to walk your pet without its leash.

When your dog is six months old, you can take it to obedience training school. In obedience classes sponsored by the American Kennel Club, owners learn how to train their pets. Owners are taught to use patience as well as firmness in training. They learn the importance of praising the animal after it has done a good job or shown progress with a difficult exercise. By learning to use voice commands and silent hand signals, dog owners eventually can put their pets through seven difficult exercises in obedience trial competitions.

Weeks of schooling and practice are necessary to prepare a dog for obedience trials. But the effort is worthwhile. Your dog should have obedience training even if you do not intend to enter it in dog shows. A well-trained dog is a pleasure to own because it has good manners. It will not bother people while they eat. It will stay off the furniture. It will not run out the door every time someone opens it. It will not bark unnecessarily. And it will not bite or growl. A well-trained dog is a valuable addition to the family.

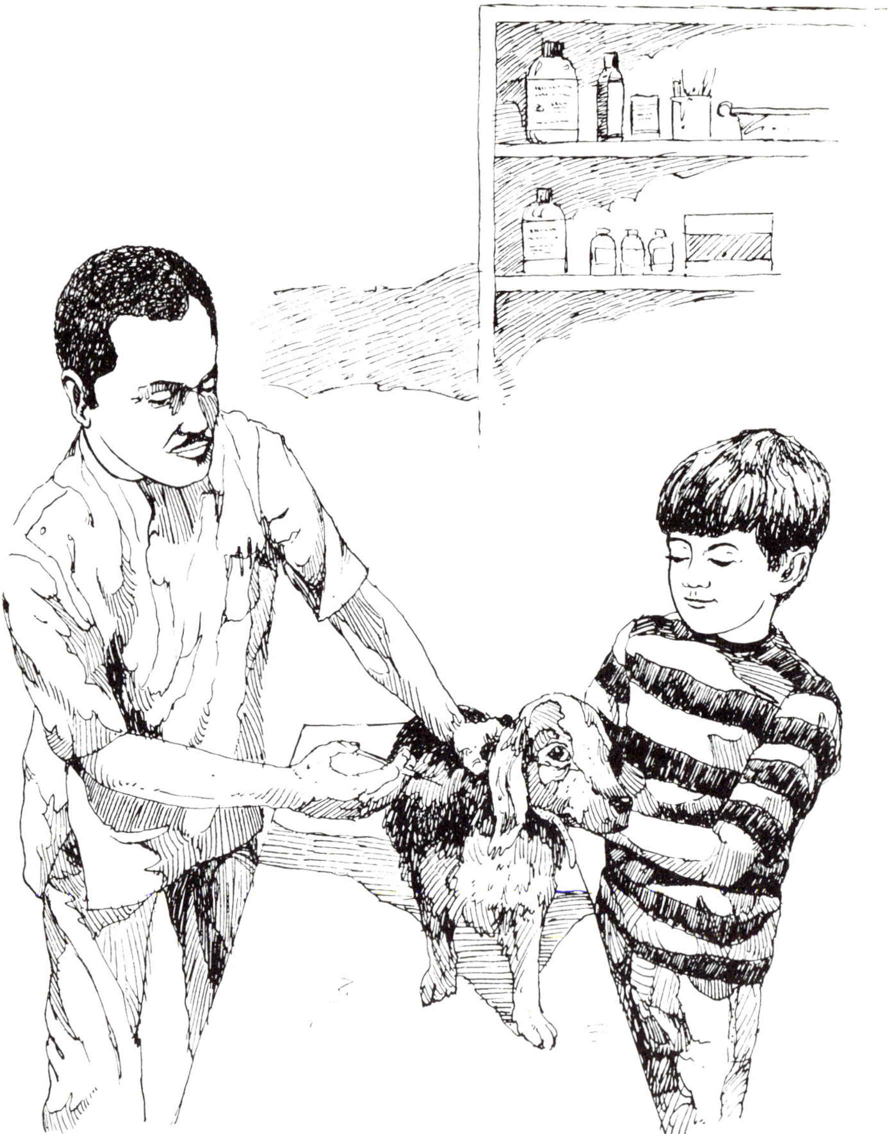

YOUR DOG'S HEALTH

Your veterinarian will be a good friend to your dog. Veterinarians are people who have gone to school a long time to learn how to become doctors of animal medicine. Their pet hospitals are much like the hospitals you and I go to. They have all the modern equipment and medication necessary to treat your pet's ailments.

At the pet hospital, the veterinarian can x-ray your dog or test its urine and blood with special laboratory equipment. By examining a sample of your dog's blood, the veterinarian can quickly diagnose an illness and prescribe the proper treatment. If your dog needs surgery, the veterinarian has a well-equipped animal operating room. Whenever your dog is sick, injured, or in need of a vaccination, take it to the veterinarian.

Be sure that your dog is vaccinated against distemper, hepatitis, and rabies. The shots for rabies protect not only your dog from this disease but also anyone whom your dog may bite. When the veterinarian gives your dog its yearly booster shot, he or she will give you a metal tag showing the date the shot was given. This tag should be attached to your pet's collar.

The veterinarian probably will check your dog for worms. These little animals, called "parasites," live inside a dog's body. There are several kinds of parasites, including hookworms, roundworms, heartworms, whipworms, and tapeworms. These parasites are found in puppies more often than in adult dogs. Worms, however, can be controlled by the medication that your animal doctor prescribes.

Other kinds of parasites can attack your dog's skin and fur. Common external parasites are fleas, ticks, mites, and lice. If your dog spends a lot of time scratching, it may be infected with one of these parasites. Powders, soaps, and sprays that kill these pests can be bought at a pet shop, or your veterinarian can supply

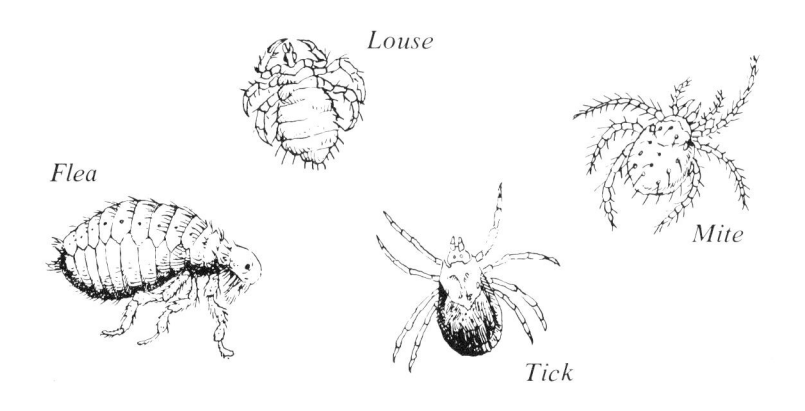

Louse

Flea

Mite

Tick

them. Your dog and its living quarters should be treated with these products frequently. Commercial flea collars are also helpful.

These external parasites are dangerous because they spread disease. The eggs of tapeworms, for example, are carried by fleas. Clean, well-groomed dogs are usually free of fleas, lice, and mites. See that your dog does not come in contact with animals that may be carrying these parasites. Still other disease-carrying parasites are ticks. Your dog can pick up ticks from trees, shrubbery, and tall grass. Ticks are larger than the other parasites and can be seen if you look through your dog's fur. Special tick sprays and powders are available to control them.

Once in a while your dog may eat grass, an action that will cause it to throw up. This is nature's way of dealing with an upset stomach. It is a normal reaction and no cause for worry. A dog also may vomit just before its mealtime. This is caused by a build-up of acid in the dog's empty stomach. This, too, is natural and of no concern. It can be prevented by keeping a dish of dry dog food available at all times. But continuous vomiting by an otherwise healthy animal is a symptom of a serious problem. It may mean that a bone or some other object is stuck in the dog's throat or that it has swallowed poison. A quick visit to the veterinarian is in order.

Other symptoms of a sick dog are: changes in daily routine such as loss of appetite and frequent naps; hiding in dark places; a runny nose or watery eyes; loose bowel movements, or mucus or blood in the stool; difficulty in getting up and lying down; lumps on the body; and open sores. Contrary to popular opinion, a cool wet nose does not necessarily mean that your dog is healthy. If it has any of the above symptoms, take it to your veterinarian. He or she will help you to nurse your pet back to health.

To safeguard your dog's health, make sure that it gets plenty of exercise. Daily exercise will give your pet a good appetite as well as keep its weight down. A brisk walk is good not only for your dog but also for you.

To further insure your pet's health and safety, you should probably keep it on a leash while it is outside. Your dog could be stolen, poisoned, or hit by a car if allowed to run free. Besides, letting your dog run free shows bad manners. To allow your dog to dirty a neighbor's yard or to frighten people who are afraid of dogs is not considerate. Depending on where you live, the law may force you to keep your dog on a leash. Leashing laws are intended to protect the health and property of all citizens as well as the safety and well-being of your pet.

FEEDING YOUR DOG

Dogs will eat just about anything. They love ice cream, steak and chicken bones, buttered toast, cheese, and popcorn. These foods, however, are not good for your pet. Dogs should have balanced diets containing all the vitamins and minerals necessary for building strong, lean bodies. Commercial dog foods supply these nutrients.

There are three kinds of commercial dog food—canned, semimoist, and dry. Many dog owners believe that canned dog food is made out of meat and that dry dog food is made out of cereal. This is not so. All three kinds of dog food are basically alike except for the amount of water they contain. Most canned dog food is made up of meat protein, fats, carbohydrates, and water. Dry dog food also contains meat protein, fats, and carbohydrates, but most of the water has been taken out. Dry dog food comes in boxes and large sacks. It can be fed dry alongside a bowl of water, or water can be poured over the food. The semimoist food comes in packets and should be served next to a dish of water.

You will have to decide which kind of food is best for you and your dog. I prefer the dry food that comes in pellets. I always keep my dog's bowl filled with this food, and I provide a good supply of fresh water alongside. My dog eats as much as he wants whenever he gets hungry. This is called the self-feeding method. It has many advantages. Dogs do not usually overeat on dry dog food. Thus, the food does not have to be rationed, or measured. The animal is properly fed even if its master must be away from home for a short time. No scheduled feeding time is necessary. Acids do not build up in the stomach of the self-fed dog. Dry food does not spoil, nor does it require refrigeration. And, when purchased in large bags, dry dog food is much less expensive than canned or semimoist food.

GROOMING YOUR DOG

Grooming your dog can be a pleasant experience for both you and your pet. If grooming is started early in your dog's life, it will look forward to these periods of closeness. The animal somehow will sense that what you are doing is for its own good. Train your dog to stand on a bench or table while it is being groomed. This will prepare it for visits to the veterinarian, where it must stand very still on the examining table.

While these sessions are intended mainly for grooming your dog, they also provide an opportunity for you to examine your pet. Check its toenails. If they are long, they should be trimmed or filed. Your veterinarian will show you the correct way to do this. Examine your dog's ears. Look for tiny specks stuck to the hairs inside the ear. These may be the eggs of lice or mites. They should be removed. If the inside of the ear appears red, feels hot, and has a bad odor, the dog may have an infected ear and should be taken to the veterinarian. Examine the dog's body for lumps, sores, and parasites also.

Long-haired dogs should be brushed and combed once a day. Short-haired dogs need this treatment only two or three times a week. Combing and brushing will usually keep your dog clean. But when the dog gets dirty from mud and grease or rolls in a bad-smelling substance, give it a bath. The bathtub, a laundry tub, or a dishpan will work nicely, depending on the size of your dog. Be sure the temperature of the bath water is around 100 degrees Fahrenheit (38 degrees Celsius). Any good soap will do. Even your own deodorant soap can be used on your dog. If the dog has fleas, you will need a special flea-killing shampoo. It is important that you rinse your dog completely so that no soap is left in its coat. After the bath, rub the dog with clean towels and keep it indoors until it is dry.

Bathe your dog only when necessary. Too many baths can remove the natural oils from the dog's coat, causing dry skin. The dog's fur is very much like a blanket. It holds in heat and keeps out cold. But this insulating feature of the dog's coat does not work when it is wet, which is why most dogs shiver during their baths. At these times dogs are very susceptible to colds. Care must be taken to keep them warm and out of drafts until they are completely dry.

In the spring of the year many dogs shed their heavy winter coats. The dead hairs in their fur should be removed before they get on your rugs and furniture. If combing does not remove them, try rubbing your dog's coat and skin with your fingers. This action usually loosens the hairs. They can then be picked up with a brush or by a stroke of your hand.

Dogs like to be clean. They enjoy being groomed and cared for. And a clean dog is a pleasure to have in your home.

WHEN YOUR DOG HAS PUPPIES

The birth of puppies is a happy and unforgettable experience. It is an excellent opportunity for the whole family to witness the miracle of birth.

If you want your female dog to have puppies, you must arrange for her to mate during her "period of heat." A female dog has such periods at about six-month intervals, and it is only at these times that she is interested in mating. Each period lasts from 18 to 21 days. During this time the female dog's urine has a very strong odor. This odor attracts male dogs and tells them that the female is ready to mate.

A female dog can have puppies when she is just six months old, but it is better to wait until she is a year and a half before having her bred. At that age the female is better prepared for the job of raising a family. If you do not want your dog to have puppies, keep her away from male dogs during her heat periods. Spayed females do not have heat periods and, of course, cannot have puppies.

Puppies are born 58 to 63 days after mating. An expectant mother dog likes to give birth in a cozy box called a "whelping box." This box probably gives the mother a feeling of security and privacy. It keeps the babies close together and makes it easier for her to feed them and to keep them warm. A whelping box should be constructed of half-inch (1.25 centimeters) plywood. For a medium-sized dog the box should be about 20 inches high, 24 inches wide, and 32 inches long (50 centimeters high, 60 centimeters wide, 80 centimeters long). A door 9 inches wide and 14 inches high (22.5 centimeters wide, 35 centimeters high) should be cut into one wall. The door should be at least 5 inches (12.5 centimeters) above the floor. This will allow the mother to walk into the box and prevent the puppies from walking out.

For miniature and small dogs a simple cardboard box will do. It should be just big enough for the mother to stretch out full length. Three sides of the box should be 8 to 10 inches (20 to 25 centimeters) high. The fourth side should be cut down to about 4 inches (10 centimeters). The whelping box should be placed in a warm, quiet place.

The first signs that your dog is going to have puppies will appear about five weeks after mating. The dog's nipples will enlarge and her stomach will widen. This is a good time to take your dog to the veterinarian for a complete examination. The veterinarian will see that your dog is in good health and will tell you how to care for her and what to expect when the puppies arrive.

From that time until she gives birth, the expectant mother will need special attention. She should be fed cooked eggs, milk, and meat along with her regular diet. She should not be allowed to jump or run up and down stairs. Frequent walks will give her the exercise she needs. And she must be kept warm and dry. Do not bathe her during her pregnancy.

About a week before the puppies are due, the dog will become restless and begin looking for a safe place to have her babies. That is the time to introduce the whelping box. Put her blanket or other bedding material into the box. This will help her get used to her temporary home. A few days before the pups arrive, remove her blanket from the whelping box and replace it with several layers of flat newspapers. You will know that the puppies are on the way when she begins to shred the newspapers and build a nest.

At this time nature takes over. The average litter has one to six puppies. Each puppy arrives enclosed in a membrane sac, which the mother dog opens with her teeth. Attached to each puppy is an umbilical (uhm-BILL-uh-cul) cord. Through this umbilical cord the puppy receives nourishment while inside its mother's body. After giving birth, the mother dog bites through this cord. Then she eats the membrane sac. This is nature's way of providing the mother with the energy she needs during the birth process. She will then carefully clean her puppies by licking them. Instinctively the puppies will crawl to their mother's nipples and start nursing. The miracle of birth is completed.

Now that the hard work of giving birth is over, the mother will probably be tired and hungry. Food should be brought to her, because she may not want to leave her litter. Give her all she wants to eat so that she will have plenty of energy to provide milk for her babies.

The first week after birth is very important to the puppies. They must be kept warm. The room they are in should be quiet and dimly lit—too much light will hurt the puppies' eyes. During this first week, do not allow any visitors to see the puppies—only members of your family. Strangers or a gang of children may disturb or frighten the mother dog, who will be very protective of her pups. But she probably won't be frightened if you change the paper in the whelping box and clean her. Approach her only if she allows it. But do not handle the pups more than is necessary.

The pups are born deaf and their eyes are closed, but they will open their eyes about 10 days after birth. For the first few weeks the mother will clean up after her babies. From then on you will have to keep the whelping box clean. The mother will nurse her babies for three to six weeks, depending upon the dog's breed and the size of the litter. Soon the puppies will start eating solid food and take less milk from their mother. This shows that they are ready to leave their mother. At this time, you can find good homes for the pups. When your dog's duties as a mother are completed, she will return to being a beloved house pet and companion.

CONCLUSION

In spite of all the love and good care you give your pet, it will someday die. The death of a dog is perhaps the only real grief that comes from owning one. But death is a part of life. Though the dog who has been a good friend will be missed, its owner can take comfort in knowing that it had lots of love and a good home.

Later, when the sadness is almost gone and only good memories are left, the human who has learned to love one dog is ready to get a new dog and begin a new relationship. And this new relationship will provide companionship, comfort, and love, just as the old one did.

INDEX

adaptability of dog, 7
advantages of owning a dog, 20
American Kennel Club, 12, 13, 16, 23

bathing a dog, 54, 57
birth, 56-58
breeds of dogs, 13-17
brushing and combing, 55

Canidae, 8
companionship of dog, 7, 20, 30, 61
controlled mating, 10-12
Cynodictis, 8

dam, 22
death of a pet, 60-61
"den method," 38-39
disadvantages of owning a dog, 17
dog shows, 12-13, 24

exercise, importance of, 48, 57

feeding: during adult life, 50-51; during puppyhood, 32; during pregnancy, 57

grooming, 47, 52-55

half-breeds, 22
heat periods, 56
heeling, 42
hounds, 13
housebreaking, 30, 33, 36-39

illness, symptoms of, 48
instincts, 7, 36, 38

jackals, 8-10

lapdog. *See* toy dogs
leashing laws, 49
litter, 58

manners, 41, 43, 49
mating, 56
Miacis, 8
mixed-breeds, 22-26
mongrels. *See* mixed-breeds

neutering, 27-28
newborn pups, treatment of, 59
non-sporting dogs, 16
nursing, 58, 60

obedience training school, 39
obedience trials, 13
origin of dog, 8-10

parasites: external, 46-48; internal, 46
pedigrees, 21, 23
puppy fat, 32
purebreds, 23-24

responsibilities of dog ownership, 30

"sealing of the bond," 30
selective breeding. *See* controlled mating

self-feeding method, 51
shedding, 54-55
silent commands, 40
sire, 22
spaying, 26
sporting dogs, 13

terriers, 16
Tomarctus, 8
toy dogs, 12, 16, 24
training, 33-34, 39-43
traits of dogs, 12

umbilical cord, 58

vaccinations, 35, 45-46
veterinarian, 35, 45-46, 57
vomiting, 48

weaning, 28, 35, 60
whelping box, 56-57, 58, 59, 60
wolves, 10
working dogs, 10-12, 13

You and Your Pet:

AQUARIUM PETS

BIRDS

CATS

DOGS

HORSES

RODENTS AND RABBITS

TERRARIUM PETS

We specialize in publishing quality books for young people. For a complete list please write

LERNER PUBLICATIONS COMPANY
241 First Avenue North, Minneapolis, Minnesota 55401